Come and join me . . .

on a folk art journey. We will visit four different countries, and I hope you will feel like you are a part of each one.

First we will visit Germany, and paint the bold, happy flowers of Bavaria, where gaily-painted window boxes overflow from spring until fall.

Then on to Sweden, and Dalarna, where my great-grandmother lived. This is where they decorated their homes by painting whole walls with colorful scenes from the Bible or special events from their lives.

Our next stop is Norway, the home of my ancestors. We'll paint the beautiful, soft-colored floral designs of Osterdalen, Oppdal, and Valdres.

Last, we will visit Switzerland and paint the elegant Swiss Rococco, with its shell-like scrolls and elegant roses.

Each of these areas are unique, yet related, but as you will see, one folk art leads to another. Now it is time for your journey to begin.

Vaer sa god!
Bobbie

Table of Contents

Willkommen to Germany!

This is one of my favorite places. I think of the Black Forest, Tegernsee, King Ludwig's Castle, walking in the rain in loden coats, capes, and hats with feathers. Love it! And the painted houses of Oberammergau, plus the painted furniture in so many of the places we stayed.

The Palette for all the pieces is: LIQUITEX jar acrylics: Titanium White, Yellow Oxide, Cadmium Red Medium, Hooker's Green, Cadmium Yellow Medium and Burnt Umber. Heavy antiquing gives each piece a warm, old look. I used OLD MASTER'S Antiquing Glaze in Natural Walnut and varnished with FULLER O'BRIEN's Pen-chrome Polyurethane. The brushes used are: LIQUITEX Kolinsky Sable Round, Series 5000 #5, LOEW-CORNELL's Liner, Series 7350 #2, LOEW-CORNELL's Flat Wash, Series 7550 ¾ inch, Poly-foam brushes.

Bavarian Plate

Plates with brightly colored rims often decorate the walls of German homes, giving them the cozy, "Gemutlich", feeling they are so known for.

Rose:

1. Fill in flower form with Cad. Red M.
2. Fill ½ brush with Cad. Red M. and other ½ with B. U. Paint a U-shape at base of flower with dark color at outside edge.
3. Fill in open top-center of rose with B. U.
4. Fill ½ brush with Cad. Red M. and other ½ with T. White. Paint each petal, keeping the white to the outside edge, filling brush with fresh paint as you need it. Using the same method, paint around center and curve down to bottom center of the rose.
5. Pick up Y. O. on tip of brush and paint a dot in the center of inner circle. Surround with T. White dots to form a flower.

Tulip:

1. Paint sides and then center with s-strokes of Y. O.
2. Feather short strokes of a mixture of Cad. Red M. and B. U. from tips of tulip downward.

Rosebuds:

1. Fill in circle with Cad. Red M.
2. Base of bud is H. G.
3. S-strokes of H. G. over bud. Add a little Y. O. to green on one side as a highlight.

Leaves:

1. S-strokes of H. G. on ½ of leaf, other ½ add some Y. O. to make a lighter green.
2. Make short slashes on one side of leaf with H. G. Outline the other side with H. G.

Rim:

1. C-strokes or curved teardrops of Y. O.
2. Paint inner part with c-strokes of B. U.
3. Overlay c-strokes of T. White on outer edge.

Finishing:

1. Antique, leaving it darker on outside edges.
2. Varnish.

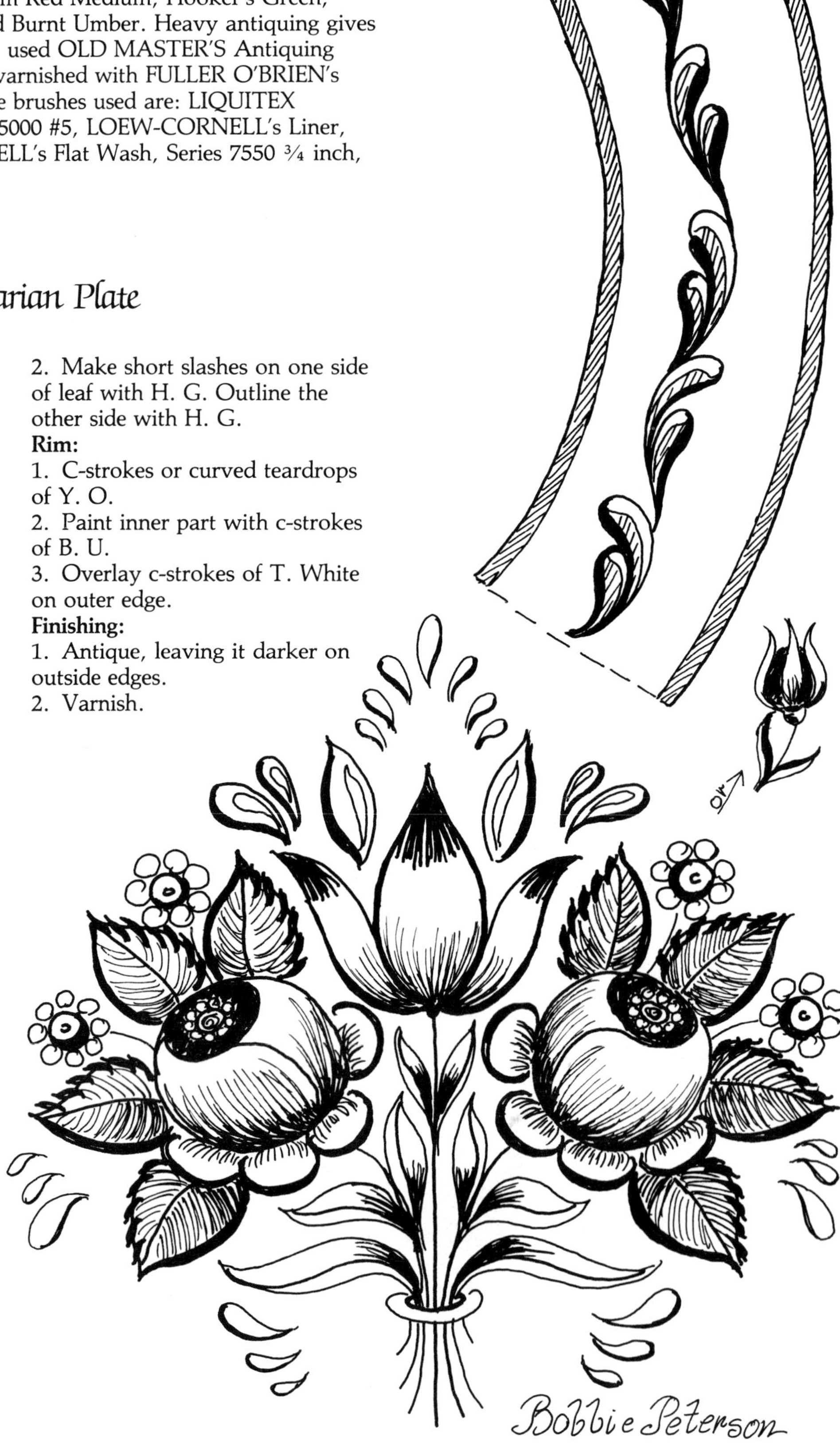

2

Oberammergau Tulip Bucket

Set a glass within our Bavarian Bucket, fill it with water and it is perfect for a beautiful bouquet of red and white tulips or any fresh flowers of your choice. The Bucket is from Cabin Craft, 402 Orange St., P.O. Box 1218, Redlands, CA 92373.

Background: FULLER O'BRIEN's Latex Semi-Gloss Ocean Green.

Rose, Rosebuds and Leaves: Same procedures as in Bavarian plate, except that T. White is used to outline leaves.

Carnation:

1. Fill in U-shape with B. U.
2. Flower cup is H. G.
3. With filbert brush, paint strokes of Y. O. around top of B. U. U-shape. Paint another below this, adding White to Y. O. Add more White to next row, ending with a stroke or two of pure White.
4. Paint stem and s-stroke leaves of H. G. Add Y. O. strokes for hi-light.
5. Bouquet is tied together with a stroke of Y. O.

Scrolls:

1. C-strokes frame the flower bouquet. First paint one large c-stroke and another within it. Paint thin strokes of B. U. within each c-stroke. Overlay with T. White strokes.

Finishing: Antique bucket heavily, leaving center of insert much lighter. Insert could be painted an off-white.

2. Varnish.

Rottach-Egern Umbrella Stand

Right inside the door of each little shop, you will find an umbrella stand or "schirmstander". On a rainy day, everyone who comes through the door puts their umbrella in, and it's there when they leave! I have one in my hall too. So I always know where to find an umbrella. Here's one for you, very similar to the one in a candy shop in Rottach. Umbrella stands are hard to find, but Pipka, P. O. Box 313, Sister Bay, WI 54234 does have them from time to time.

Background: Stand: CREATIVE ACRYLIC's Carriage Red. Insert and Inside: CARVER TRIPP's Vanilla.

Rose, Tulip and Rosebuds: Same procedure as in Bavarian plate.

Daisy:

1. Petals: With Liquitex #5 brush stroke in petals of Phthalo Blue and T. White, starting at the back and working forward to front, adding more white as you go along.
2. Center: Fill in with Y. O. Add a stroke of Cad. Red M. to bottom and blend upward. Hi-light top with a stroke of Cad. Y. M. Add dots of T. White on bottom side.

Bow: Phthalo Blue with T. White added to top part and straight lines for under part of bow.

Leaves and Stems: H. G. stems and small leaves. Add Y. O. to green for one side of leaf, keeping the other side darker. Outline with H. G.

Scrolls: Same procedure as described in Tulip Bucket.

Finishing:

1. Antique heavily, leaving white insert lighter.
2. Varnish.

Umbrella Stand Handle

4

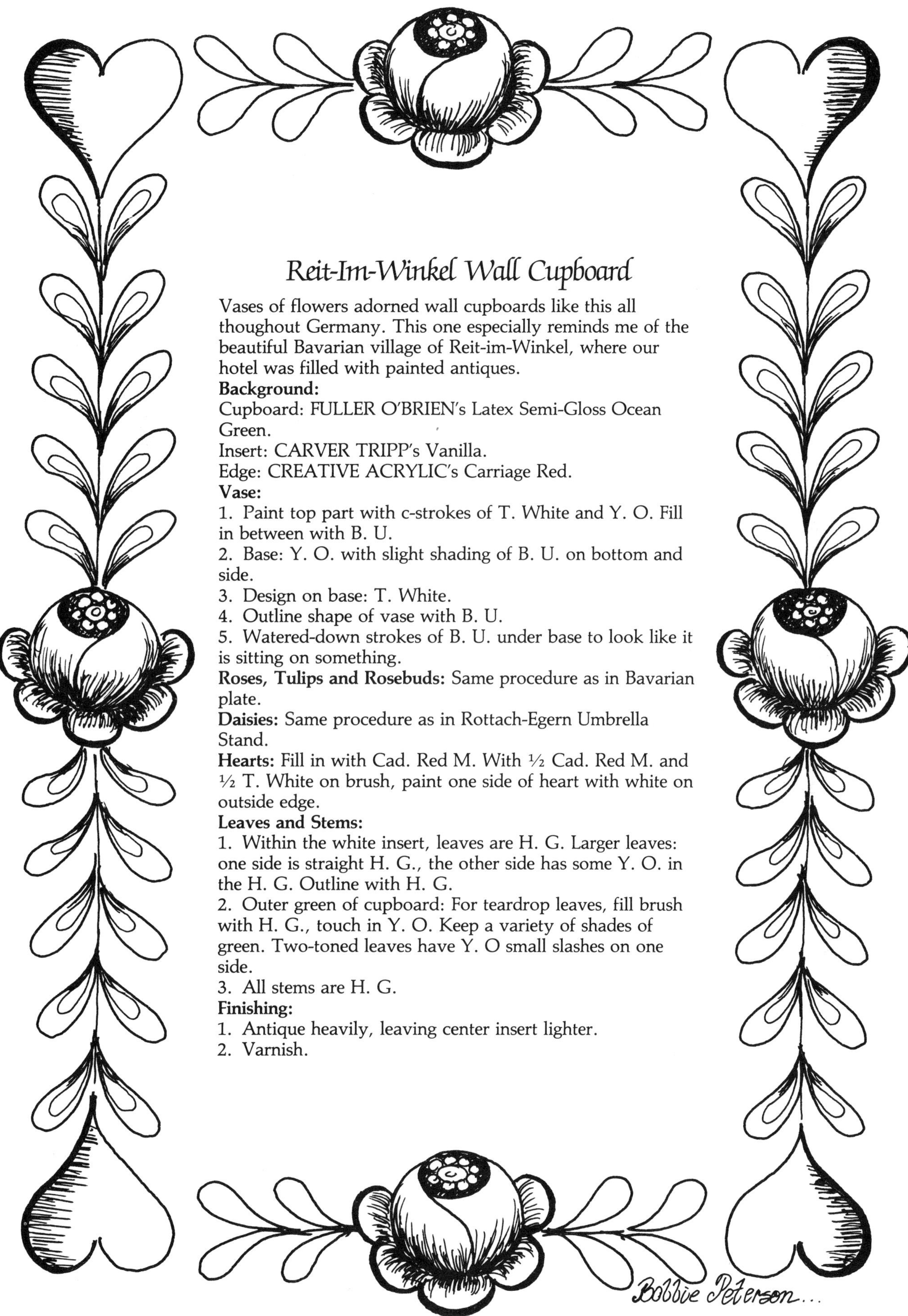

Reit-Im-Winkel Wall Cupboard

Vases of flowers adorned wall cupboards like this all thoughout Germany. This one especially reminds me of the beautiful Bavarian village of Reit-im-Winkel, where our hotel was filled with painted antiques.

Background:

Cupboard: FULLER O'BRIEN's Latex Semi-Gloss Ocean Green.

Insert: CARVER TRIPP's Vanilla.

Edge: CREATIVE ACRYLIC's Carriage Red.

Vase:

1. Paint top part with c-strokes of T. White and Y. O. Fill in between with B. U.

2. Base: Y. O. with slight shading of B. U. on bottom and side.

3. Design on base: T. White.

4. Outline shape of vase with B. U.

5. Watered-down strokes of B. U. under base to look like it is sitting on something.

Roses, Tulips and Rosebuds: Same procedure as in Bavarian plate.

Daisies: Same procedure as in Rottach-Egern Umbrella Stand.

Hearts: Fill in with Cad. Red M. With ½ Cad. Red M. and ½ T. White on brush, paint one side of heart with white on outside edge.

Leaves and Stems:

1. Within the white insert, leaves are H. G. Larger leaves: one side is straight H. G., the other side has some Y. O. in the H. G. Outline with H. G.

2. Outer green of cupboard: For teardrop leaves, fill brush with H. G., touch in Y. O. Keep a variety of shades of green. Two-toned leaves have Y. O small slashes on one side.

3. All stems are H. G.

Finishing:

1. Antique heavily, leaving center insert lighter.

2. Varnish.

Bobbie Peterson...

Black Forest House

Deep in the Black Forest, houses with huge thatch-covered roofs dot the country-side. During the summer, their window boxes abound with flowers. We went inside a house just like this in Schwarzwald in the Gutach Valley.

Background: Stain with OLD MASTER's Pecan Antiquing Glaze.

Roof: Paint short strokes with filbert brush across the bottom and work upward painting with LIQUITEX's H. G., adding a little Cad. Y. M. now and then to the brush for variety.

Window:
1. With flat brush, fill in with B. U.
2. Outline window frames with off-white.

Stone: Either side of door, dab in with B. U. and T. White.

Pots and Wheels: T. White and B. U. to make off-white. Paint area back of pots and wheels B. U.

Outlining: With B. U. liner brush outline windows, balcony, door, etc.

Flower Boxes: H. G. leaves. Dots of Cad. Red M.

Sign: Lettering is B. U. Edges are B. U.

Finishing: Varnish.

Black Forest Couple

The huge red pom-poms on the hats of the Schwarzwald women and the neat black suits with bright red lapels and vests are the colorful costume of the Black Forest. CERAMCOAT acrylics are used throughout.

Bobbie Peterson...

Välkommen to Sweden!

My great-grandmother, Christina, was born in Applebu, Darlarna, and had an inn along the King's Highway. So I feel a special kinship to Dala painting. My teachers, Hans Prins, who painted in the same style and manner as the old Dala painters did, and Bengt Engman, who painted with whimsey and a fresh approach, brought this all alive to me.

I have used CERAMCOAT acrylics for all the Dala painting because they give the clear, soft colors I was looking for.

The Palette is: Straw, Hallingdal Red, Blue Spruce, Black-green, Ivory, Gamal Green, Salem Green and Burnt Umber. For brushes, I used LIQUITEX's Kolinsky Sable Round, Series 5000 #5, LOEW-CORNELL's Liner, Series 7350 #2, LOEW-CORNELL's Filbert, Series 7500 #4 and #6, LOEW-CORNELL's Flat Wash, Series 7550, ¾ inch for backgroundings, antiquing and varnishing. The varnish is FULLER O'BRIEN's Pen-Chrome Polyurethane.

Hälsingland Trunk

Each child in Sweden often had their own barnaskorna to keep their special possessions in. This twin-heart design has the date on one side and the initials on the other.

Background:
Trunk: CERAMCOAT's Hallingdal Red.
Inserts: CERAMCOAT's Blue Spruce.

Leaves:
1. The four outside leaves of the top design are Salem Green. On one side with your liner brush, paint a line following the curve of the leaf form. Outside line is Ivory and another line inside of Straw.
2. The four inside leaves are Gamal Green with lines of Ivory and Straw.

Red Roses:
1. Undercoat top and bottom roses with Ivory, then paint Hallingdal Red.
2. Top circle of rose is Blue Spruce.
3. Dot in center is Straw.
4. With liner brush, outline circle and each petal with Ivory.
5. Paint 3 curved lines within the rose Ivory, followed by lines of Blue Spruce. Outline bottom of rose with Blue Spruce.

White Roses:
1. Paint 2 side roses Ivory, paint as many coats as necessary to cover.
2. Top circle of rose is Blue Spruce.
3. Dot in center is Straw.
4. Outline circle and each petal with Hallingdal Red.
5. Paint 3 curved lines within the rose Hallingdal Red, followed by lines of Blue Spruce. Outline bottom of rose with Blue Spruce.

Center Design:
1. Circle flowers of Ivory.
2. Center is Straw.
3. Dot of Hallingdal Red inside Straw center.
4. Fern Leaf is Blue Spruce with strokes of Gamal Green underneath.

Twin Hearts:
1. Undercoat with Ivory.
2. Paint Hallingdal Red, as many coats as necessary to cover.
3. Outline with Ivory.
4. Dates and initials inside with Ivory and Blue Spruce.

Circle Flowers:
1. Undercoat with Ivory.
2. Paint Hallingdal Red.
3. Dot at top center of Straw.
4. Leaves and stems are Ivory.

Finishing:
1. Antique with OLD MASTER's Antiquing Glaze in Natural Walnut.
2. Varnish.

Svepta Box

These oval boxes served many purposes, such as, sewing items, trinkets or ribbons. Often they were given as a betrothal gift, and filled with carved things made for the bride by her intended. Box available from Cabin Craft (Refer to pg. 3).

Background: CARVER TRIPP's Vanilla.

Center Flower:

1. Paint circle Hallingdal Red with filbert brush #6, leaving center open.
2. Paint 5 petals of Hallingdal Red inside circle.
3. Outline shapes of petals and inside short lines with Black-green.
4. Dots of Straw within inner circle.

Side Flowers:

1. Paint circle Straw with filbert brush, leaving center open.
2. Paint bottom 5 petals with second coat of Straw.
3. Outline shapes of petals and inside short lines with Black-green.

4. Center: 2 coats of Straw, stroke of Hallingdal Red at bottom on center, cross-hatch and outline in Black-green.

Top Leaves: Blue Spruce, Ivory scrolls inside, then outlined with Black-green.

Blue Shade Center:

1. Paint triangle between scroll and flowers Blue Spruce.
2. While still wet, paint Ivory down center and then blend outward.
3. Cross-hatch with Black-green.
4. Dot within each square is a mixture of Ivory and Blue Spruce to make a very light blue.

Scroll:

1. Stroke of Straw at top.
2. Next a stroke of Ivory.
3. Blend into Blue Spruce, ending with darkest Blue Spruce at scalloped edge.
4. Ivory vein lines.
5. Outline with Black-green.

Two-Toned Leaves:
1. S-stroke of Straw, 2 coats to cover.
2. Under s-stroke of Blue Spruce.
3. Outline in Black-green.

Vase:
1. Paint with Blue Spruce.
2. While still wet, paint Ivory down center and blend outward.
3. Inner design is Hallingdal Red with c-strokes of Ivory within.
4. Cross-hatch and outline vase shape in Black-green.
5. Lt. blue dots.

Top of Vase:
1. Paint Blue Spruce.
2. While still wet, paint Ivory down center and blend outward.
3. Paint 3 strokes of Ivory for design within.
4. Paint 3 petals of Hallingdal Red at top and bottom, 2 coats if necessary.
5. Outline with Black-green.

Handles:
1. S-stroke of Straw.
2. Stroke of Hallingdal Red on inside.
3. Outline with Black-green.

Oval Flowers:
1. Fill in with 2 coats of Straw. Blend in Hallingdal Red on underside.
2. Cross-hatch, dots and outline in Black-green.

Small Flowers:
1. Paint circles of Straw.
2. Outline petals in Black-green.
3. Centers in Hallingdal Red.
4. Leaves and stems are Blue Spruce.

Finishing:
1. Outline outside edge of oval box with Blue Spruce.
2. Sides of top lid: Water down Blue Spruce. Paint a small portion at a time with a flat brush. While still wet, hit with side of your hand every half inch to form a pattern. Paint a small portion again and repeat along the side.
3. Varnish.

Applebu Foot Stool

I am decorating our guest room in the Swedish style. Already I
have a very old child's bed from Dalarna that I treasure. Many of
these painted pieces will look beautiful in this room, especially
this stool. Available at Viking Woodcrafts, 1317 8th S.E.,
Waseca, MN 56093.

Liebe
Welcome
Willkommen

Välkommen
Välkommen
86

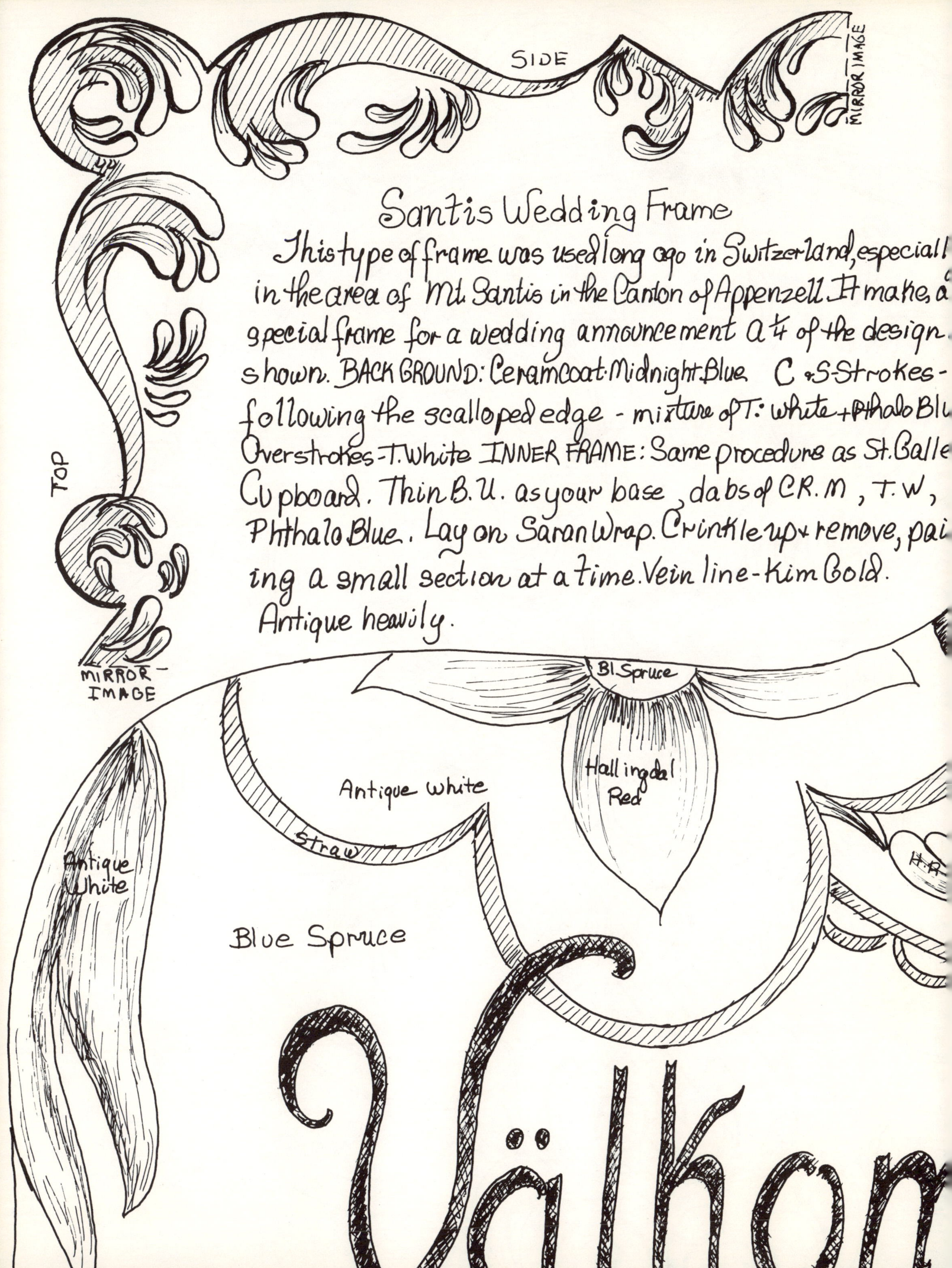

SIDE
MIRROR IMAGE
TOP
MIRROR IMAGE

Santis Wedding Frame
This type of frame was used long ago in Switzerland, especially
in the area of Mt. Santis in the Canton of Appenzell. It makes a
special frame for a wedding announcement a 4 of the design
shown. BACKGROUND: Ceramcoat Midnight Blue   C & S-Strokes-
following the scalloped edge - mixture of T. white + Phthalo Blue
Overstrokes - T. White INNER FRAME: Same procedure as St. Galle
Cupboard. Thin B.U. as your base, dabs of CR.M, T.W,
Phthalo Blue. Lay on Saran Wrap. Crinkle up & remove, pai
ing a small section at a time. Vein line - Kim Gold.
Antique heavily.

Bl. Spruce
Antique white
Hallingdal
Red
Straw
Antique
White
H.R
Blue Spruce
Välkom

Bobbie Peterson

Paint on shutter

Scalloped Plate
al style of rosemaling
as inspired by Knut
rne, Oppdal. Background
Blue Spruce. White
wer: Soft White.
ue. with Soft White dots,
enter. Red Flowers:
ith white overlay.
Blue Side Flowers:
DK Blue drawn out
. DK. Blue. Soft
d. Dot flowers: CYM
enter. Berries: Soft
t w with CRL. DK
 each berry. Ferns:
KBlue. Leaves: DK.
lay with Lt. Blue.
Blue outlines scallop.
Soft White CYM center.
 Antique with
ut. Stipple outer
 with thinned DK Blue.

son ....

MIRROR IMAGE

straw

Heart within a Heart
A Bavarian Welcome Heart to put right outs
door! Available at Cabin Craft. Background: Fuller O
Roses: Same as Bavarian Plate except - add 2 ex
Leaves: 2 shades H.G. Outline with T. White.
Umbrella Stand. Cross-hatching - T. White.
Background: Carver - Tripp's - Vanilla - Scroll
Tulip Bucket.   Welcome: Ho

MIRROR IMAGE

BU
T.W.
CRM
T.W.
CYM
T.W.
CRM
T.W.
HG
CRM
T.W.
Black.
Flesh tow
BU
T.W.
CR
CYM
T.W.
T.W.
Black
Twin Roses
paint right on
the announcement.
Swiss Couple
cut out of
light card-
board +
glue on.
Antique
White
DALA HORSE
Hallingdal Red
Straw
Straw
Blue Spruce
Straw
Straw
S
HR
S
HR
Antique White
Straw.
men
Welcome for the heart within a heart.
Welcome
Round Trinket Box
This is painted especially
for your dresser to hold your
Norwegian jewelry in. Box

Appenzeller Cheeseboard

This huge cheeseboard would hold a round of cheese like the ones we saw being made in Stein. The cheese factory shone with cleanliness. It was located in the rolling hillside of Appenzell. The cheeseboard is available at Cabin Craft.

Background: Ceramcoat Midnight Blue.

Rose: Same procedure as Luzerner Sugar Scoop.

Leaves: Same, except that c-strokes are a mixture of T. white + Pthalo Blu → Lt. Blue.

Tulips: Center - Cad. R. M. One side ; T. white + Cad. R. M → Lighter red. Other side - Cad. R. M + B. U. → darker red. Top ; Stroke with Light, thin lines of T. white downward. Dot at base - C. Y. M.

Small Flowers; Cad. R. M. with H. G. half moon, Cad. Y. M. dot. Dots; T. white around center. Strokes: H. G. + T. White → Lighter green. H. G. under. Over lay with T. White. Scroll; Pthalo Blue + T. W. → Light Blue. Outer edge; 3 small c-strokes across outer edge. Outline with T. White. Dry brush w/ T. W. Paint line of Lt. Blue inside, darker blue within, over lay with white. Vase ; Cross-hatch with Lt. Blue. Dots - T. White. C-strokes - Lt. Blue to form outer edge, overlay with T. W. Top Scroll; C-strokes - Lt. Blue. Overlay with T. W. Thin line of Lt. Blue around design. Antique heavily, leaving inner design lighter.

Tegernsee Window Box

All through Bavaria you will find flower boxes overflowing. Painted shutters frame the lace-curtained windows. This Tegernsee window is a bright addition to your Kitchen, and the flowers will bloom throughout the year. Background: Frame-Ocean Green. Window: Bamel Green. Window Box - Pecan Stain.

Curtains: Watered down T. White. Outline curtain edge and folds with T. White. Paint scrolls on curtain with T. White to look like lace. Blossoms: Top petals -T. White+YO→H. Yellow, Bottom petals-more YO in them. Center-YO blilight with CY. M. Dots - H.G -Window Box - available through Cabin Craft.

Antique White
Blue Haze
front
Ocean Green
of T. White
same as
de Heart:
me as
Green
301-1st St. Decorah, Iowa 52101
Background: FolkART's Robin Egg • Flowers, Leaves, Stems: Same as in Østerdalen Tine. Berries: CAL. Shade with DK Blue. CAL. dot. Finishing: Stipple with DK Blue mixture leaving center lighter.
Bobbie Peterson

Gerta-Willy
Germany
Christina-Carl
Sweden
Anny-Rolf
Switzerland
Brita-Björn
Norway

Swedish House

Red Buildings with white trim and red tiled roofs are often found in the villages of Sweden. They look like gaily painted pavilions.

Background: CERAMCOAT's Hallingdal Red.

Trim: Ivory around house, windows and door.

Roof: Paint rows of scallops across of B. U., looking like tiles.

Windows: Blue Spruce.

Door: Watered down B. U. Outlined in B. U.

Flowers: Gamal Green stems and leaves, dot of Blue and Ivory.

Sign: Background in Ivory. Trim with Hallingdal Red. Lettering in Blue Spruce.

Finishing: Varnish.

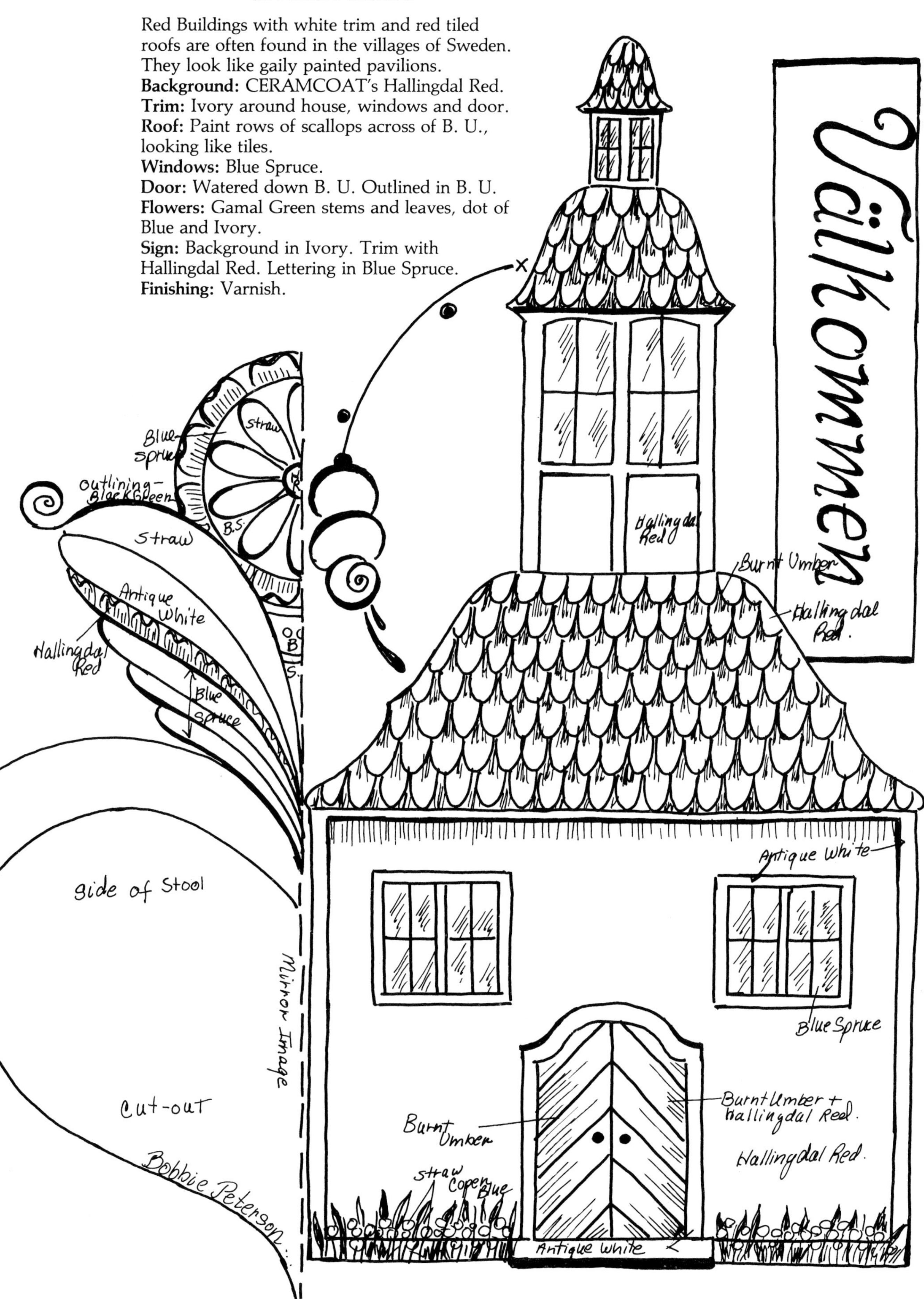

Swedish Couple

This is the costume of Dalarna. His jaunty red hat and her gay striped apron give a very festive look. I really love the Swedish colors and style of painting. CERAMCOAT acrylics are used.

Velkommen to Norway!

I've studied twice in Norway, the first time at Rauland in the Telemark Valley, and last summer in Molde on the West Coast. We visited every museum we could, plus many private homes. We were privileged to study with Norway's finest rosemalers.

We will paint the beautiful floral designs and soft colors of Oppdal, Osterdalen and Valdres. In our designs, I used the traditional oil paints and kept my palette limited, using soft whites, reds, peach tones, and the blue-greens of these areas. All of the background colors are acrylic and are followed by a coat of CERAMCOAT waterbase varnish to give them a soft sheen for easier mobility of the brush stroke.

The Brushes Are:
1. Winsor-Newton Round sable Series 7 #3.
2. Winsor-Newton Round sable Series 3A #2.
3. LOEW-CORNELL Filbert Series 7500 #4.
4. LOEW-CORNELL Flat Series 7300 #4.

The Palette is Liquitex Oil Paints:
1. Soft white: Titanium White, a little Raw Umber and a little yellow Ochre.
2. Soft red: Cadmium Red Light, a little Burnt Umber, Yellow Ochre, and Titanium White.
3. Dark red: Add Alizarin Crimson to the above mixture.
4. Dark Blue-green: ½ Prussian Blue, ½ Burnt Umber, a little Yellow Ochre and a little Cadmium Red Light.
5. Bright yellow: Cadmium Yellow Medium.
6. Gold: Yellow Ochre.
7. Burnt Umber.

Also needed are paint thinner, linseed oil, and PRATT LAMBERT Clear Finish Varnish.

Valdres Breadboards

This is one of my favorite styles of rosemaling. I have a huge cupboard in our bedroom that I've painted with a scene of hills and trees of blue in the background. The foreground has sprays of roses and tulips. The two bottom drawers have 3 bouquets across them, just like the designs on the breadboards.

Background:
1. Stain with OLD MASTER's Pecan.
2. Paint front with CERAMCOAT Robin Egg.

Tulips:
1. Base with Dk. Red mixture.
2. Paint s-strokes of soft white. Take fresh paint with each stroke.

Blossom:
1. Paint outer circle of Dk. Red.
2. With #3 filbert brush paint petals of Off-White.
3. Fill in center with B. U.
4. Dots of Cad. Y. M. in center.
5. Dashes of Cad. Y. M. touched in Cad. Red M. around center dots.

Ruffled Flowers:
1. Paint in flower form with Dk. Red.
2. Center is B. U.
3. Fill #4 or #6 flat brush with Dk. Red, edge with Off-White, paint ruffles around center. Take fresh paint for each ruffle downward.
4. Dots of Cad. Y. M. in center of B. U. Add a few dots of Cad. Red M. at base.

Dot Flowers: Dk. Red with Gold center.
Berries: Dk. Red with Gold dot at top.
Leaves:
1. Paint with Dk. Blue mixture.

2. Fill round brush with linseed oil and paint stroke along bottom side of leaves.

Ground:

1. Paint Dk. Blue.

2. At top either add White to Dk. Blue or add linseed oil to brush.

Finishing:

1. Stipple lightly with Dk. Blue mixture around center design.

2. Let dry and varnish.

Tine

A tine is used in Norway to carr[...] Small pressure strokes of Soft White across
When we attended a Midsummer [...] [fl]owers. Painting rows downward, softly
Celebration last June, our hosts b[...] [sh]ading into red at base. Use worksheet as your
a tine. We picnicked on the rocks [...] [gui]de.
Sea and watched the sun that neve[...] **[Ste]ms:**
down. Tine is available through C[...] [F]ill in with Gold.
Refer to pg. 3. [...] [P]aint a stroke of Soft Red across the top.

Background: [...] [O]utline bottom with Dk. Blue.

1. FOLK ART's Robin Egg. **[Leav]es and Stems:** Dk. Blue
2. Varnish with CERAMCOAT wat[...] **[Antiqu]ing:**

White Flowers: [...] [Ad]d paint thinner and linseed oil to Dk. Blue
Paint petals at the top Soft White usi[...] [mixtu]re to use to antique the tine, leaving flower
filbert brush. As you go around, add [...] lighter.
Red so that the petals are a little dark[...] [Wit]h Dk. Blue thinned mixture, paint edging
bottom. [...] the cover, handle and ends. With
2. Base of flower: Soft Red with Dk. [...] [crinkl]ed saran wrap, twist and turn to give a
bottom. [...] look.
3. Center is Dk. Blue.
4. Dots of Bright Yellow. 3. Let dry thoroughly and varnish.

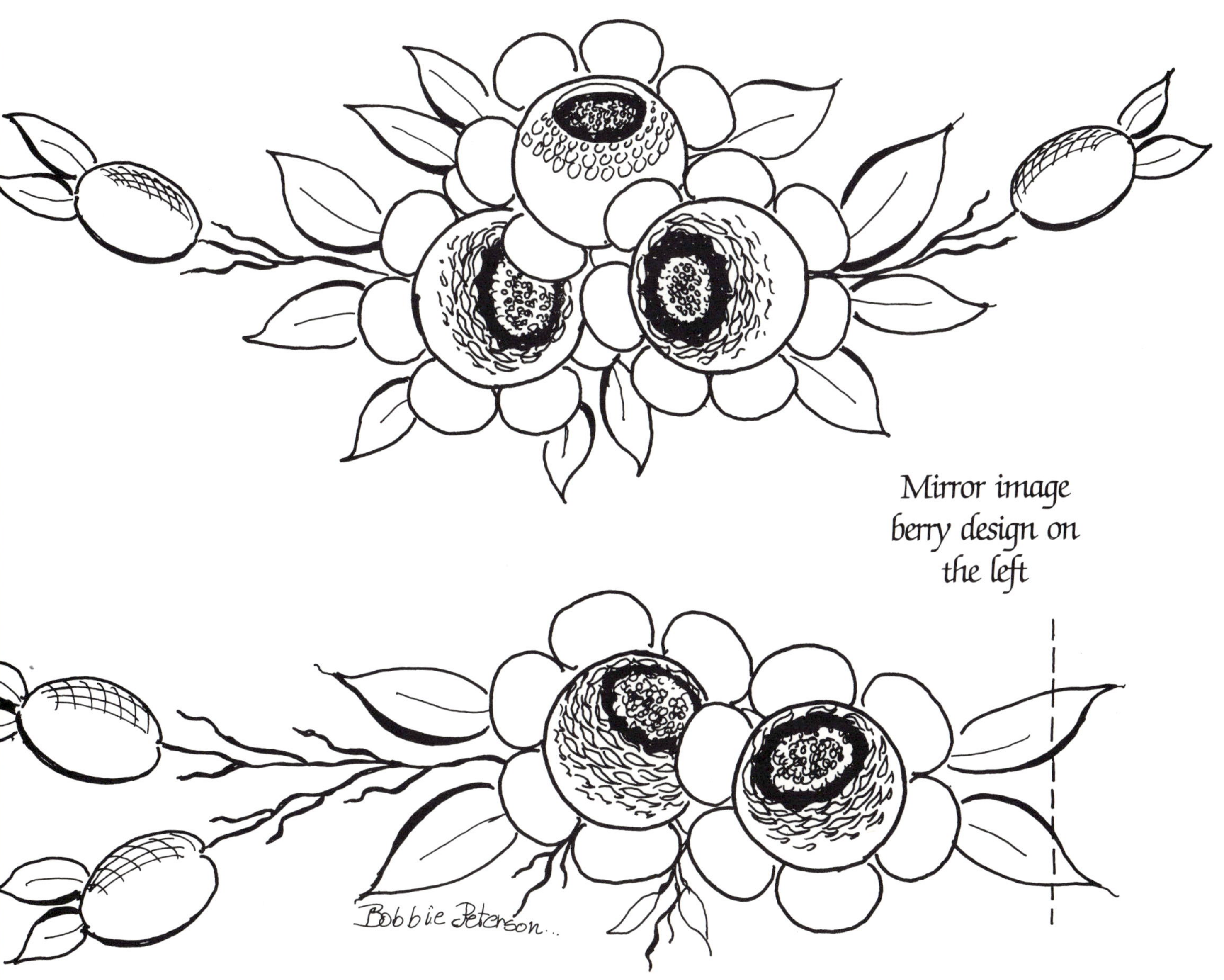

Mirror image
berry design on
the left

Bobbie Peterson

Osterdalen Cupboard

This design was inspired by a huge secretary
with baskets and vases of flowers on the doors.
I love the soft, yet rich colors.
Background: CERAMCOAT's Salem Green.
Rim — Adobe.
Basket:

1. Add linseed oil to B. U. and paint shape of
basket.
2. Paint slashes of Gold down center and
middle of sides.
3. With flat brush, paint strokes to simulate
weaving across the basket, strokes becoming
smaller as you paint downward.
4. Hi-light with Off-White one side.
5. Base and Handles: Paint B. U., overstroke
with Soft White teardrops.

Top Flower:
1. With #4 filbert brush, paint top 4 petals,
adding a little more White to the Soft Red.
2. Bottom 2 petals paint Soft Red.
3. Center is Dk. Blue.
4. Dot flowers of Soft White, center dot Yellow
Ochre.

2nd Flower: Same procedure as in Osterdalen
Tine, except that above center circle is a half-
moon of Soft White, add only 2 rows of Soft
White dabs surrounding lower part of inner
circle.

3 Bottom Flowers: Same procedure as in
Osterdalen Tine, except that the petals on the 2
outer flowers are a rosier, Off-White. This is for
contrast.

Buds: Double load flat brush with Soft White
and Soft Red, and paint a half circle.

Dot Flowers: Soft White dots with Soft Red
centers.

Leaves: Dk. Blue, outlined on one side with Soft
White.

Flowers on Back of Cupboard: Same procedure
as in Osterdalen Tine.

Finishing:
1. Under basket stroke B. U. across lightly so
that basket looks like it is sitting on something.
2. Stipple all around Flower Basket design with
Dk. Blue.
3. Varnish.

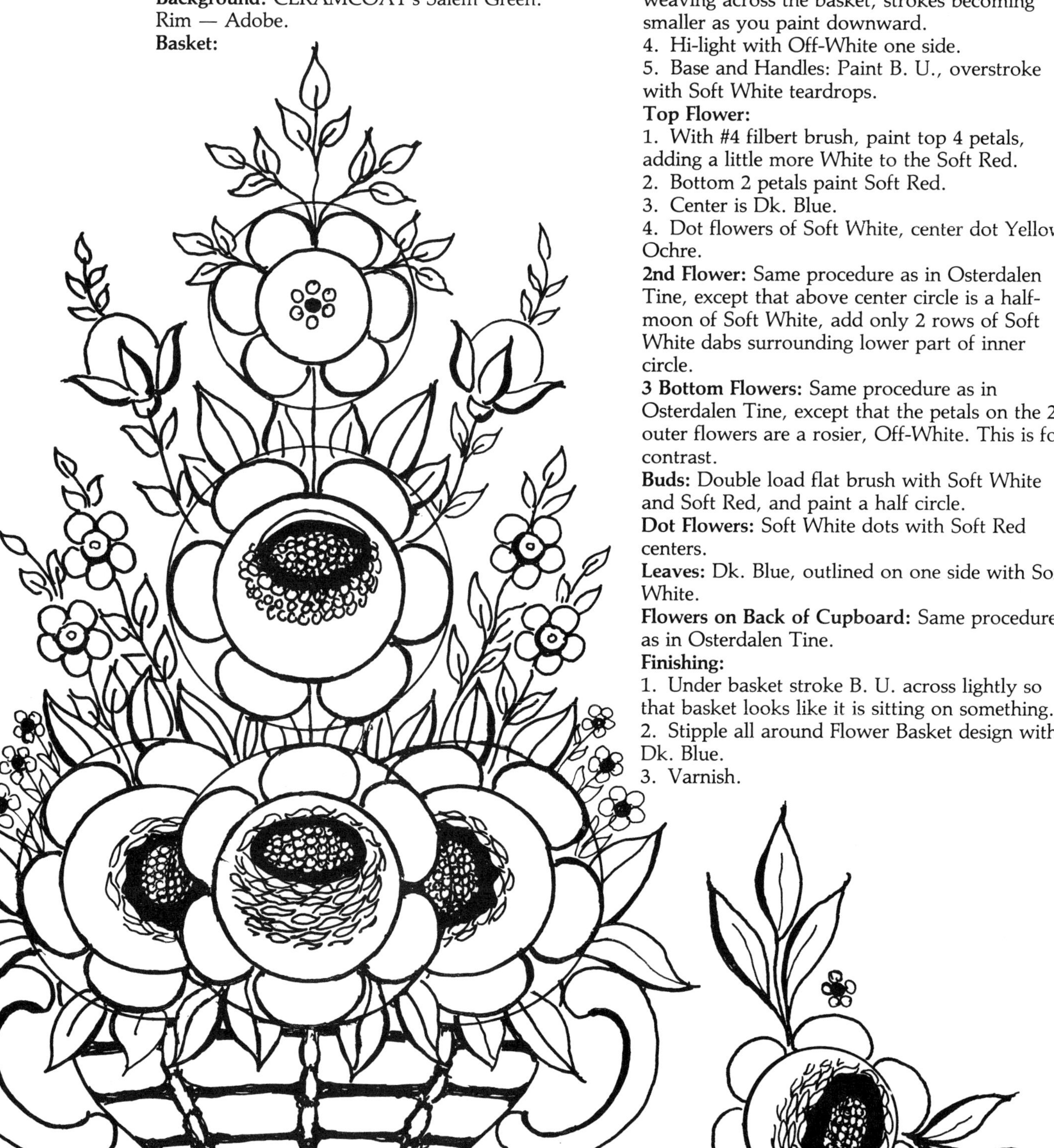

Norwegian Stabbur

This is one of the most unique buildings of the Norwegian countryside. It is used for storage. The lower floor was for smoked meat, fish and grain and the second floor for storage of valuable family possessions. During the summer, it served as a guest room. In Telemark, especially, each farm has a stabbur, each one more picturesque than the next.

Background: OLD MASTER's Pecan Antiquing Glaze.

Door: Paint diagonals of B. U.; door knob: Cad. Y. M.

Windows: B. U.

Flowers: Green leaves and stems. Dots of Cad. Red M. and Cad. Y. M. for flowers.

Outline: Follow pattern as guide and outline wood, posts, doorway, ladder, stairs, scallops below roof line with B. U.; outline with Dk. Blue front posts, log ends, and stair tops.

Finishing: Varnish.

Norwegian Couple

This is the wedding costume or bunad of the beautiful Hardanger area where some of my ancestors came from, so this has special meaning to me. The Hardanger Fjord is breathtaking, each side is filled with orchards of apples, plums and pears. Imagine how beautiful it is in the spring time!

Paint with CERAMCOAT acrylics.

Gruetzi From Switzerland!

There is a special feeling about the Swiss Alps that is universal. Everyone is drawn to the beauty of the craggy mountains and quaint villages. I've been to Switzerland many times, visiting folk museums, and even getting up at 4:30 a.m. to see the famed "Alpfahrt", when the Swiss bring the cows up the mountains to the summer pastures. It was an experience of a lifetime to see the gaily dressed men lead freshly groomed cows, with the huge bells, up the mountains. We stood along the roadside with the Swiss village and farm folks to watch and admire them.

In our Swiss painting, we'll concentrate on the Rococo style. This is one of my favorites of all the folk arts. Our palette is LIQUITEX jar acrylics: Titanium White, Cadmium Yellow Medium, Yellow Oxide, Cadmium Red Medium, Hooker's Green and Burnt Umber. I used OLD MASTER's Antiquing Glaze in Natural Walnut and varnished with FULLER O'BRIEN's Pen-chrome Polyurethane.

Brushes:

1. LIQUITEX's Kolinsky sable round, Series 5000 #5.
2. LOEW-CORNELL's Shader flat, Series 7300 #4 and #6.
3. LOEW-CORNELL's Flat wash, Series 7550, ¾ inch or Poly-foam brushes for backgrounding, antiquing and varnishing.

Alpen Heart

The heart is a favorite in the Alpine area. It is a symbol of love throughout the world. We will paint two favorites of Swiss Folk Art, the star flower and the carnation.

Background: CERAMCOAT's Salem Green. Edge: Cad. R. M.

Carnations: Cad. Red M. Slashes of T. White, B. U.

Star Flowers: Cad. Red M. — red flower. CERAMCOAT's Blue Spruce — blue flower. Outline top — T. White, bottom — B. U.

Leaves: H. G. — strokes of Cad. Y. M., H. G. on each side.

Scrolls: T. White and B. U. as your base. Use color worksheet as your guide.

Finishing: Antique, heavier on edge. Varnish.

Luzerner Sugar Scoop

When we visited a folk museum overlooking the city of Luzerne, the kitchen was filled with wood-carved utensils hanging on the walls. This could have been one of them.

Background:

1. Inside: OLD MASTER's Antiquing Glaze in Natural Walnut.
2. Outside and Handle: CERAMCOAT's Salem Green.

Roses:

1. Circle and petals: C. R. M. Center: B. U.
2. Fill Brush with ½ C. R. M. and ½ B. U. Stroke around base, blending upward.
3. Fill brush with C. R. M., edge with T. W. Paint around B. U. center. Paint another stroke below it, another across the bottom, curving up in the middle.
4. B. U. center: 3 strokes C. R. M.; edged with T. W. Dots: C. Y. M.
5. Petals: C. R. M. Inside: shaded with B. U. Outline: T. W.

Small Flower: C. R. M. Dots: T. W.

Leaves:

1. Paint ½ H. G. and other ½ lighter green.
2. Center vein: H. G.
3. Small strokes: one side H. G., other side C. Y. M.

Small Leaves: H. G. Veins and outlines: C. Y. M.

Finishing:

1. Triple load #6 flat brush, fill with CERAMCOAT's Salem Green, one side with CERAMCOAT's Ivory, the other with water. Paint stripes all along inside edge of scoop, filling brush with fresh paint, as necessary.
2. Antique, leaving inner areas lighter.
3. Varnish.

Swiss House

This house can be seen in the village of Stein am Rhein, which is the best-preserved medieval town in Switzerland. It is just one of the many houses with rococo scrolls and scenes painted on them that line the village square.

St. Gallen Cupboard

There were no closets as we know them, and so, huge cupboards called schranks were used for storage. They were decorated with paintings, such as scenes of the owner's life, gorgeous flowers and fruits, scrolls, and then, they marbelized, striped, and used many finishing techniques to give them a very sumptuous look. Our cupboard is a small version of this schrank. It is available at the Norwegian-American Museum, Decorah, Iowa.

Brushes:

1. LIQUITEX's Kolinsky sable round, Series 5000 #5.

2. LOEW-CORNELL's flat wash, Series 7550, ¾ inch or Poly-foam brushes for staining, antiquing and varnishing.

Background: OLD MASTER's Pecan Antiquing Glaze and Stain.

Red Roses: Same procedure as in Luzerner Sugar Scoop.

White Roses: Same procedure as Red Roses, except that T. White and B. U. are mixed to make an Off-White. This is your main color. Then edge with T. White as in Red Roses.

Small Flowers: Same procedure as Luzerner Sugar Scoop.

Leaves: Same procedure as Luzerner Sugar Scoop.

Small Leaves: Paint half H. G. and half a mixture of H. G. and Cad. Y. M. to make a lighter green. Outline with H. G.

Finishing:

1. Top Ridge: With #6 flat brush, alternate stripes of Cad. Red M. and B. U. diagonally across to center, blending into each other. Then paint with same color stripes diagonally the other direction meeting in the center.

2. Base and Frame: Paint about a 6-inch portion at a time, as acrylics dry very fast! With flat brush, paint a watered down B. U. on just that portion. While it is wet, quickly paint in dabs of Cad. Red M. and dabs of B. U. here and there. Quickly lay saran wrap over. Now it will not dry and you can crinkle it up. The paint will move together, forming the marbelized look. Lift up the paper, and go on to the next 6 inches. Repeat all around edge and the base. Then paint thin jagged lines and v's of CERAMCOAT's Kim Gold to look like veins.

3. Drawer and Top Area: Paint in OLD MASTER's Natural Walnut Antiquing Glaze. While still wet, take soft paper toweling, twisted, and wipe circle shapes to give it sort of a tortoise look.

4. Antiquing: Antique center sections of rose design with OLD MASTER's Natural Walnut, rubbing off lightly rose and leaf area. Antique knobs heavily.

Swiss Rococco Plate

The most beautiful Swiss Rococco of all is in a home that is now a museum in Ebnat Kappel. The flowers, scrolls and vases are similar to the design of this plate.

Background: OLD MASTER's Natural Walnut.
Red and White Roses, Leaves, Small Flowers, Scrolls: Follow color worksheet.
Vase:
1. Fill in basic shape with mixture of T. White and B. U. to make an Off-White.
2. Fill brush with Off-White mixture, edge in T. White. Paint left side of vase and c-strokes on lower part.
3. Fill brush with Off-White mixture, edge in B. U. Paint right side of vase and strokes on lower right part.
4. Fill in strokes with B. U., outline left side with T. White.
5. Paint strokes of Off-White in top part and at lower two parts of vase. Outline top and hi-light left side with T. White. Outline bottom part with B. U. Outline small circle in bottom scallop of vase, T. White and B. U.

Finishing:
1. Antique lightly.
2. Stipple edges by painting around rim with OLD MASTER's Natural Walnut and dabbing with crumbled up saran wrap.
3. Varnish.